WINNING FROM START TO FINISH

WRITTEN BY

YAMUEL BRADLEY

WINNING FROM START TO FINISH

****

YAMUEL BRADLEY

Editorial Consultants: Heather Pendley, developmental editor from reedsy.com, Allen Taylor, chief content officer @Taylored Content LLC.

Other books by Yamuel Bradley

A Lover's Guide to Happiness

A Lover's Guide to Happiness Increased

Love Letters in Text

Get Your Head Out of Your A**

Self Published by Yamuel Bradley

Winning From Start to Finish

ISBN

Paperback:978-1-7378951-0-7

Hardcover: 978-1-7378951-1-4

ebook:978-1-7378951-2-1

To receive discounts for bulk orders contact:

Dieauka Y Bradley Sr.

1-253-248-9897 or yamuel818@gmail.com

Contents

Introduction

Winning from Start to Finish begins with discipline. You will hear a lot of people say "motivation is the key to success." Yamuel Bradley has put together a masterpiece on how to power your motivation and ambition with discipline. Motivation gives you a vision that can change at any time. Discipline and ambition gives you a purpose and helps you reach a designed goal.

Yamuel Bradley's youth was not easy, but the tragedies he faced influenced this book. Although raised by his loving grandmother, Yamuel still longed for a close relationship with his parents. He was never able to experience this connection with his mother, who was brutally murdered by her boyfriend when Yamuel was only 12 years old.

Losing his mother left a hole in Yamuel's heart so big that he began to make poor decisions as a teenager that greatly impacted his life. With no positive male role models to guide him in the principles of being a responsible man, Yamuel found himself caught up in the dangerous world of sex, drugs, and crime. He had been sent to juvenile facilities multiple times by the time he was 18, and was in and out of prison until the age of 40.

Yamuel hit rock bottom while serving his last stint in prison, and began to grasp how much his actions had negatively impacted not only him, but others too—like his grandmother and his own children. With this new revelation, Yamuel began to pray and meditate, seeking God for guidance. He asked God to forgive his past actions and to help him change his heart and mind to become a better man.

Yamuel spent his time in prison writing the thoughts and emotions he harbored from his experiences, finally able to release them. He realized how his absence from the lives of his children could ultimately result in them making poor decisions just as he had. Taking the initiative to break the cycle, Yamuel reached out to his children, and their response brought him great joy and the motivation that inspired his literary works.

After serving his time, Yamuel had an entirely new outlook on life. He learned not only the power of a sound mind and pure heart, but the power of forgiveness. A brand-new man, Yamuel reached out to his father to help him write, but most of all, in helping his own children. This reunion was a guiding force for Yamuel as a parent.

However, with a fresh start and reunifications came unfortunate loss. In 2006, he lost his grandmother, the one woman who had supported him all his life. Following her death, his oldest daughter, Julia, passed away unexpectedly at age 28.

The two losses crushed Yamuel's soul with extreme guilt and pain for not making better decisions and being present when he could. Unprepared for the loss of a child, Yamuel had difficulty coping with his daughter's death and felt himself drowning in grief to the extent he could barely function from day to day.

With his family by his side providing love and support, and his father's influential words *never stop being the best you*, Yamuel didn't allow his loss to alter the positive changes he had worked so hard for. Instead, he expressed his guilt and pain from those tragic events in writing while continuing to move forward.

Because of his struggles, Yamuel sought direction from successful professionals. Through their guidance and stories, Yamuel implemented the steps in this book, enabling him to go from earning $30,000 a year to almost $200,000 a year with room to grow.

Nothing happens in life until you make it happen. In this book, Yamuel speaks of the many challenges you will come against, preparing you for any failures that may arise on the job, in relationships, or in business and finances.

You will find yourself invigorated with the determination to succeed in everything you set out to do, and the understanding of how you are responsible for your own change.

When you take the steps outlined in this book, all self-doubt will fade away and you will learn how to attain the success you desire and life you deserve. You will become focused, and nothing will distract you from the purpose God has for you.

As you read this book, your passion to attain transition skills and develop your self-worth will increase. You will be able to stand up with confidence and stop putting more time and effort into your job than into yourself. You must believe that before your day begins, your victory is already won.

You must care about everything you do from here on out to see results. Whatever else you have going on in your life no longer matters. The time to let go of everything that has been holding you back and succeed is *now*.

"He who is not courageous enough to take risks will accomplish nothing in life."

-Muhammad Ali

CHAPTER 1

- - - - - - - - - - - - - -

You determine your quality of life.

How often have you gone through the day asking yourself, Why am I still in the same position as yesterday? You have goals in mind, but you just can't get there. Every day is played out over and over, the same as the day before: Work, kids, gym, Netflix, or Facebooking while the kids play games on their phones, Nintendo, Xbox, etc. The same routines repeat themselves day after day with no real traction in achieving your goals.

It's not what happens that determines your quality of life. Rather, it is what you do.

The sun rises and sets every day. And, like the sun shining on all of us, certain things are also experienced by everyone. You can't get stuck thinking about how events in your life are unfair, as if you were the only person to have experienced them. Dwelling on the past or current disappointments means you are not focused on the future.

Here are some questions you must ask yourself:

- What areas of my life do I really want to improve right now?
- How is my job going?
- Is my relationship with my significant other a good one?
- How are other family relationships doing?
- Am I satisfied with my physical appearance?
- How about the spiritual side of my life? Am I happy with it?

To make any progress, you'll need to identify what you want to improve, how you plan to improve it, and the steps necessary to achieve your goals. No one can do this for you; if you are waiting for someone to walk into your life and make it better, you will wait for eternity because that is not likely to happen.

Winning from Start to Finish is about how you can bounce back from disappointment, a guide to help you focus on changing your mindset from accepting failure as your destiny to expecting success. Adjusting from loss and moving forward is the focus of every successful person.

Too many people walk around saying, *I* should *do this,* or *I* should *have done that.* But they only interest themselves in the basic skills of survival, such as paying the light bill or filling the refrigerator with food. They somehow expect to work less and make more money while having more time to enjoy life. Sorry, but that is not how it works.

Many people look at what others are doing and say, *I want to do what they are doing*, but don't take the necessary steps to get where that individual is. Why is that?

One reason is because if they don't receive the response they are looking for, they get discouraged. If they aren't laughed at, they are placated. With a pat on the shoulder, a friend may say, *You can't do that! You must learn to crawl before you can walk. Be more realistic.*

Instead of standing up for what they believe, the dreamer says, *Yeah, you're right, but wouldn't it be nice?* They give up before they get started.

Why can't you do what other people are doing or become what other people are becoming? Only because you have allowed yourself to believe it is impossible.

You are the key to making things happen in your life.

When you told yourself that you want to follow in someone else's footsteps, it was because you saw something good, profitable, and exciting. More importantly, you knew your talents and abilities. You believed in your own thoughts and intentions. You could see yourself doing them.

This could be anything, from advancing your career aspirations to pursuing fame as an actress or musician.

You could be a receptionist in a hospital and see a nurse working with patients and you tell yourself, *I can do that*. A nurse in a hospital watching doctors perform their duties tells herself, *I can do that*. A father watching his child's baseball game looks at the coach and says to himself, *I can do that*. Whatever your dream, you must take steps to make it a reality. No one else can do that for you.

We often allow words and thoughts to remain just that, words and thoughts. If you want to be the nurse who becomes a doctor, the father who becomes a coach, or the receptionist who becomes a nurse, you cannot passively sit by as your dreams wither. You never know what you can do until you do it.

The fear of challenging oneself to be better is an epidemic. Sadly, we create a limited vision for ourselves. We don't want to put ourselves in a position where our limited vision, skills, and abilities dictate our futures.

Remember, *you* are the key to realizing your dreams and living up to your potential. Nothing in life happens until you make it happen. People may try to discourage you; they may say you cannot succeed. Why might you allow someone to dissuade you?

Vision.

You see, the people telling you *it is impossible* do not have your vision. They believe that if *they* can't do it, then *you* can't either.

What people think about you and the likelihood of your success is none of your business. Do not allow negative energy to become toxic to your well-being. Surround yourself with people exuding positive energy. This may mean distancing yourself from a lifelong friend or family member and associating with people who have positive energy and aspire to lofty goals.

For example, the ABC Company must temporarily lay off 5,000 employees. Mark and Clarence are friends employed at the company. They both work in engineering and are told the layoff will last eight months to a year. After work one day, they go to a bar and make a plan to look for temporary, replacement jobs. The next day, they scour the want ads and apply for jobs online, but most of the positions have been filled. After several weeks of daily job searches, Clarence loses hope of finding a job. He starts hanging out at the bar more instead of looking for work. He feels defeated and argues a lot with his wife.

Mark, on the other hand, never stops looking for work. In fact, because it had been so long since he'd searched for a job, he sought assistance. After three months, Mark is hired by one of his company's competitors.

Mark did not allow the no's to be no's. Instead, he turned a no into a yes. Because of Mark's ability to see himself working and taking care of his family, he was able to secure a job.

The difference between Clarence and Mark was eyesight vs. mindset. Eyesight is judging by what you see, judging according to appearances. Mindset is how you interpret what you see.

Clarence said, There is no way I'm going to find another job and surrendered to the rejections. Mark refused to accept rejection. Instead, he pushed until a no became a yes. That was a good thing because, as it turned out, the layoff lasted for three years and some workers, like Clarence, never returned to their jobs.

You Are Responsible for Your Own Change

We can't anticipate the things that might happen in our lives. All we can do is overcome obstacles and find our own sources of inspiration. Nothing changes unless you change. You are in control of that change. If you want to make your dream come true, you must stay focused. Some people believe it is their personal business to stop you from living your dreams or would rather "get even" than get ahead. Do not allow anyone to distract you from the purpose God has for you.

A wise man once said, "Someone's opinion of you does not have to become your reality." You create your own reality.

"*The first step toward success is taken when you refuse to be a captive of the environment in which you first find yourself.*"

-Mark Caine

CHAPTER 2

. . . .

Winning from start to finish begins with discipline.

You will hear a lot of people say that motivation is the key to success. But without discipline, motivation cannot exist.

Motivation starts with inspiration to achieve something desired. Let me explain the difference between motivation and discipline: You can look in the mirror and tell yourself that you are going to start working out, so you head to the gym. Now, your motivation is to develop six-pack abs or lose weight. To achieve this goal, you must be disciplined. With motivation, you have a vision that can change at any time. But with discipline, you have a purpose and a designed goal. You must create the steps that will guide your ongoing practice along with rules of engagement.

Discipline puts you on an accelerated track toward your full development. Mastering the circumstances of your life comes through discipline. Disciplining your mind and daily activities will create more opportunities for success.

There are many glittery distractions that can remove you from the motivation you once had. Emotions can mislead you, feelings can tempt you, and thoughts may cloud your judgment. If you are disciplined in your goals you can achieve anything.

There are going to be times when you will not be motivated, but, through self-discipline, all things will be possible for you.

Great athletes are self-disciplined. Great leaders and entrepreneurs also practice self-discipline. The difference between motivation and self-discipline is that motivation can fade away. But when you are self-disciplined, you put yourself in a position to achieve success.

Kobe Bryant did not become a great basketball player because he was motivated. Barack Obama did not become president of the United States because he woke up one morning, looked in the mirror, and said *I will be president*. Jeff Bezos and Bill Gates did not reach their goals because they were *motivated*. Each one had to become *disciplined* to achieve success.

Remember, every day is a struggle. Not everything is going to be easy. You will experience trial and error, but if you are disciplined, achieving your goals will be easier.

If you fail, the mental discipline you create for yourself will not allow you to feel like a failure. It will drive you to try again. Through failure comes success.

Failure allows you to understand what not to do on the next go-round. With discipline, you will begin to look at life's circumstances differently; with an open mind, you will allow yourself to move forward.

You must understand that to bring any dream or goal to fruition, you must want to become the best version of yourself. All success starts with self-discipline. President Lincoln once said, "Discipline is choosing what you want now, and what you want most."

With discipline comes pain because you'll have to develop new routines and continue with them until they come to you naturally, as habits.

Some people say they do not have enough time, but we all have 24 hours in a day—and others find that to be enough time. Therefore, time cannot become your excuse.

The problem, not the excuse, is that the body has become disciplined before your mind, and you are not aware of the change. Your body will tell your mind that it is too tired to get out of bed, so you will find yourself unconsciously closing your eyes and resting longer than necessary. It is easy to listen to your body and surrender to its demands. But don't give in to that temptation.

When finally you get out of bed, your mind will tell you that you have overslept. You'll feel the same way you would have felt had you gotten out of bed when your mind wanted you to.

The same thing can happen with daily routines. The social structure around you can trigger an emotion and you react. But, you must not allow your body to control your mind. It is also important not to allow your social structure to take control. You must not allow your body to control your mind.

"There's a difference between interests and commitment. When you're interested in doing something, you do it only when circumstances permit. When you're committed to something, you accept no excuses, only results."

-Art Turock

CHAPTER 3

Commitment is vital to activate discipline in your life.

No excuse is acceptable when you commit to being disciplined in following a dream. If you are unable to honor a commitment to yourself, it will deplete your self-esteem; when commitment is not honored, it weakens your faith in yourself.

No one feels good when they fall short of keeping their commitments. And when your commitments to other people are not honored, you weaken your relationships with those people—whether your children, spouse, or coworkers.

The most important person your commitments should matter to is you. When you are disciplined, keeping your commitments is easy.

Let me ask you this: What would your life be like if you kept every commitment you made, with yourself and everyone else?

How do you think your life would be now if you committed to making every word you say important?

For the next 30 days, promise yourself to only make commitments that you intend to fulfill. If you honor every promise you make for 30 days, you will feel powerful. To accomplish that, you will have to be very disciplined.

If 30 days sounds too challenging, start with five days. You need to start somewhere to prove to yourself it is possible.

I started life coaching a few years ago. I did not plan to be a coach; it just fell into my lap. I was invited to a women's group and, let me tell you, I was nervous. I was going to be surrounded by women who wanted answers to life's most pressing questions and I didn't know what I was going to talk about. Before I got out of my car, I prayed to God, thanking Him for the opportunity. I practically begged Him to help me get through the evening.

I knew I had to walk into the meeting with confidence, but humbled by the opportunity. I entered the room full of chatty women and looked around, fumbling for a topic to speak on. I looked into the eyes of the women in that room and didn't see confidence. I sat down and one of the women said to me, "I work in sales, and I find myself feeling like it's me against the world. I strive to be better than everyone in the office, but feel like I'm not getting the credit I deserve."

As she spoke, I could sense that she lacked confidence. I waited for a window of opportunity then said, "To become better at something, you must train your body and your mind. Ask yourself, 'How can I approach my career now to become better at my job?'

"Losing must become exciting to you because you will see your weaknesses exposed and you can figure out how to overcome them. The most difficult thing will be to face those exposed weaknesses and initiate a plan to turn them into strengths."

That evening went well. The energy and excitement I felt in that room was awesome. I had a strong feeling the women were ready as they grew more excited about tomorrow.

We do not have all the same gifts. Get over whatever is holding you back, those things that keep you failing. When you study your craft, you will be able to adjust and improve; you will see different ways to be a better you. You must do the hard things that train your body and mind to get past the mistakes you make repeatedly. When you learn from your mistakes, you will improve yourself.

"Success is no accident. It is hard work, perseverance, learning, studying, sacrifice and most of all, love of what you are doing or learning to do."

-Pele, Brazlian soccer player

CHAPTER 4

Nobody wants to be a loser when it comes to work.

Not getting the position you applied for feels horrible. But when you don't get that position, whining, crying, and complaining about it won't change the facts.

What you should ask yourself is, *What did the other person have that made them more qualified for the position?* Follow that with, *I'll have that qualification next time.*

Most people will not ask these questions. They will complain about not getting hired, allow their emotions to get stirred up, or find themselves disliking the competition they once considered a friend. Others walk away from their job because of a bruised ego, placing their family's well-being in jeopardy. Do not let this be you. If you have a family, they must be more important than your ego.

Evaluating every situation that comes your way is important. Adjusting takes time and does not happen overnight. Remember your end game. If you don't have one, create one. Having an end game will help you make better decisions when your ego is challenged. Having an end game can help you at work when you feel defeated and want to walk out, or in school when your desire is to give up because you feel like you do not belong. There will be times when you will feel like all the work you've put in is for nothing. If you do not have a goal, these thoughts will let you walk away from success.

It is like your first day at the gym. You know the routines that can get your body in shape, and you have hard work ahead of you. You are not going to lose 20 pounds your first week at the gym. You are not going to perfect the discipline needed to succeed unless you put in regular work. If you are motivated and cultivate strong self-discipline, you will give yourself a better chance to succeed. You never want to catch yourself saying, *I wish I would have done more.*

If you have a purpose in life and are disciplined in reaching your goals, you substantially increase your chances of success. But you must work hard without expecting anyone to hand you everything.

You must set yourself on fire. Ignite a passion for something. Claim your own success and quit looking behind you or someone will pass you up. Let that thought fuel the fire to be better tomorrow than you are today.

Provide a model for your children; lead your family and friends by example. Show them that if they put in the work, their dreams can come true too.

There are going to be times when you don't feel like working because you're exhausted and don't want to push yourself, but do it anyway. This is discipline. *Empowering discipline. Focus. Achievement.*

Never give up, just keep putting one foot in front of the other. That is the path to success and something greater than your dreams will materialize as you achieve greatness.

"Every great dream begins with a dreamer. Always remember, you have within you the strength, the patience, and the passion to reach for the stars to change the world."

-Harriet Tubman

CHAPTER 5

. . . .

Why do you deserve what you want?

How many people ask themselves this question? How many have written down *why* they think they deserve what they want? Only 1 percent.

This question does not come up when creating goals or visualizing dreams. If you write down the answer to this question and review it every day, you'll discover why you are so different from everyone else and why you deserve success. Writing down your answer creates a new urgency and helps you overcome challenging moments that will arise. Become a part of that 1 percent.

Some minor life setbacks become major setbacks because we haven't answered the question, *Why do I deserve what I want?*

If you can't answer this question, then you do not deserve the success you desire.

The answer is not, *Why not me?* It is, *I deserve what I want because . . .*

Let's go! Stop creating dreams with only 50 percent motivation and 40 percent discipline.

Many of us can create beautiful dreams to change our lives if we follow through. The problem with these dreams is they stretch out too far into the future. You tell a friend, *I'm going to do such and such* and you really mean it.

The excitement in the dream is even more empowering when you have your family, coworkers, or friends behind it. But, the discipline to see the dream come true is not there for too many people. So, the same dream you had last year is still the same dream this year. However, you could have realized that success, that achievement, right now if you had been disciplined and followed through.

If you had a book for every goal you set, your neighbors would call you a hoarder because your home would be cluttered with books. The books (goals/dreams) would be everywhere and look like trash waiting to be picked up. You would receive a notice from the county to clean up the mess.

Did you know you could make every word you speak become reality? If your thoughts are negative, your days will be too. You can give yourself a bad day just by your thoughts. You can have an awesome job that other people wish they had and find yourself wishing you were not there. You must understand how powerful the mind is.

When you play negative thoughts in your mind, your attitude will become negative. You can unconsciously remove yourself from a strong position in life that could give it more meaning simply by thinking negative thoughts; thoughts control your actions.

Some pride themselves on a strong work ethic. Do you? You may see that the work ethic of people around you is poor; they do not take their job as seriously as you do. Yet, you find that management is paying more attention to them, applauding their work more than yours. In your mind, these thoughts play defeatist scenarios and you mentally complain. Those thoughts make you feel like your work is not taken seriously.

Now, when you go home to your family, you do not appreciate your job or your peers. Instead, you complain to your spouse about things neither of you can control.

A wise philosopher once said, "As you think, so shall you be." You will become what you think about, so you must be careful what you think.

Regardless of what may be going on around you, you must have positive thoughts. You must command your subconscious mind to think good thoughts.

You can overcome negative thoughts by getting up early and feeding your mind on positive thoughts. Wake up without pushing the snooze button and listen to something optimistic, then feed your body with good food that will fuel you. Look in the mirror and tell yourself, *Today is going to be an awesome day.*

Even if it's not, you can take a bad day and make it better. I have come to understand that the mind is a battlefield. Most of our battles are won, or lost, in the mind. Many people battle thoughts of failure every day and talk themselves into failure; they may be going in the right direction, but negative thoughts can destroy their happiness and change their future.

When you see someone receive something you know they don't deserve, something you have been working hard to get for yourself, your thoughts can become your enemy. Instead, applaud that person. If you do, then when you receive a raise or promotion, someone else will applaud you.

The real growth challenge comes when you have been knocked down. How you handle that determines your reality.

When bad things happen on the job, at home, or at school, some people make that one fleeting bad experience a permanent situation. They allow it to alter their life. You cannot allow moments of agony to color your entire life. Regardless of your circumstances, if your focus is on success and you continue to walk in that direction, you will find achievement and success. Do not allow your emotions to control you. Your mind automatically dwells on the negative. If you train it to think positive, when negativity does arise, your mind will redirect you to continue focusing on success. This discipline is not something you are born with—it's like a muscle that needs to be trained.

"If you continue to think the way you've always thought, you'll continue to get what you've always got."

-Kevin Trudeau

CHAPTER 6

. . . .

Selling yourself is an everyday job: for parents, school teachers, and the workforce.

To reach the next level in life, we must sell ourselves. However, because we do not review our daily goals, many of us fail to reach the pinnacle of success. Whether persuading our children that college is for them, convincing our employer that we deserve a raise, or motivating someone else to excel—success looks the same.

But if you live your life based on the opinions of others, you will find many roadblocks.

For example, one Halloween, a coworker came to work dressed as Luigi. When two other coworkers saw him, they said, "Oh, man, I wanted to dress up too!"

I asked them, "Why didn't you?" They said they thought everyone would think they were stupid for doing so. These coworkers allowed others' opinions to dictate how they'd experience celebrating a particular holiday. They put negative thoughts into their own heads, imagining that people at work would make fun of them. Their day could have been so much more enjoyable if they had not permitted the possible negative opinion of others to dictate their actions. Their fun day was lost before they walked out of their homes.

A simple redirection in your thought processes can elevate you to a different level in life. I want you to really believe this before you put this book down, because it is especially important. It is a lesson you must learn to be successful.

How many of us can say we are working as hard on ourselves as we are at our jobs? At one time, many believed in job security. We believed that the job we had at the time would be the one we retired from. However, when COVID-19 came around, many found themselves unemployed. Worse, we found that everything we had worked hard for was in jeopardy; our homes and living situation, our children's education, our car payments, our physical health. Even our relationships were affected.

You've heard "the love of money is the root of all evil," and it's true. When it is gone, everything around us began to deteriorate.

We get so comfortable with our lives that we stop developing ourselves mentally, physically, and spiritually.

You may have thought, *I have a good job so I no longer need to excel in anything.* Well, this thought process is a cancer developed by an undisciplined mind. If you do not have something in your portfolio other than your current job, it is time to create new avenues of revenue. Having additional sources of income gives a person's life more meaning and a stronger foundation. More financial security. It's called "controlling your destiny."

When you are in control of your own destiny, you no longer need to depend on your boss for a job. You don't worry about someone else's opinion of you affecting you and your family's lifestyle. When you create something you can control, you are no longer a victim of circumstances. You control how much you're worth rather than rely on someone else.

"The future belongs to those who prepare for it today."

-Malcolm X

CHAPTER 7

Grow your skills to avoid stagnation.

Have you taken a long look at the people around you? When you're in a grocery store, do you ask yourself about the life of the person pushing the cart past you? Do you believe the lifestyle you were raised with—and cultures you're so used to—have changed? Just as neighborhoods and hairstyles change, so do job requirements.

The world changes every day, and if you want to be on top, you must too—with a sense of urgency. To succeed in life, you must work hard on improving yourself and avoid stagnating. Just as you are trained to do a job proficiently, others seem to be trained to hold you down so you will not grow, to make you believe that you are not good enough for your job. They want you to stay in the warehouse making less money than you are worth.

If you won $1 million dollars, how would you feel? Accomplished? Secure? Overwhelmed by happiness and relief? Why not feel this way today?

If you won $1 million dollars, you would think about all the things you would do with your money. Each thought would be wondrous, wouldn't it? Why not experience that now? Why wait for a one-in-a-million chance when the opportunity to feel like a million bucks is here right now?

We have been groomed to *not* feel like a million bucks. We have been conditioned to believe that every day is a struggle and if we can get through the day, then we will live to fight another one. But the value of self-improvement is more than any dollar amount—even a million bucks.

Let's talk about a controlling supervisor or boss; a boss that always reminds you of his or her power. When they walk into the office, everyone acts like they are working. If you have a controlling boss, are you afraid to ask for time off because you know you will receive a long, drawn out story before receiving their "yes" or "no"?

A supervisor or business owner is supposed to create an exciting and engaging atmosphere if they want to keep employees and generate more business. However, many don't.

Most business owners get caught up in the daily grind of keeping the business afloat and forget the little people who sweat eight or more hours a day to keep their dream blossoming. That kind of job doesn't make you feel valued, does it? Of course not.

You can't use that kind of job as a stepping-stone to the next level of your career. Don't allow yourself to be walked on or passed over for another raise or promotion. Sitting still only leads to stagnation.

Instead, work on transition skills and develop your self-worth. Stop putting more time and effort into a job than you do yourself. The time to learn new skills is now.

The key to developing a sense of self-worth is focus. You need to retrain your mind by recognizing distractions that are keeping you from accomplishing your dreams. If you increase your personal presentation power, you'll control your future.

Learn new skills so you can earn the income you deserve. You are worth much more than $15, $40 or $100 an hour!

To evaluate your real self-worth, ask yourself:

- What do I have going for me that is a real plus?
- What do I need to learn for my ideas to blossom into reality?

We have to come out of the shell we have crammed ourselves into; we must acquire new skills so we can perform at a level that breeds success.

Gain new experience in your field or business and focus on what you want to become. It's like mowing your grass for the first time at your house you just moved into. Some people mow their front yard and cut the grass too low or the mower swerves around so it looks like a drunk mowed the yard. They water it on a hit-and-miss basis then wonder why the lawn looks so cruddy.

Others might first research how to make their grass greener and healthier prior to mowing the grass. They learn which products to use to kill weeds and make the grass greener. When they cut their yard, it looks awesome. The lines are perfect. But, most importantly, they water the grass to nurture and restore the lawn to its true beauty. If you could put these two yards side by side, the difference is clear: it is their level of desire to succeed at nurturing a beautiful lawn.

You must care about everything you do if you want to see results. You must research, study, and obtain the right information to be successful.

The true path to winning is laid by lessons learned from failing. You will fail—everyone does at some point. But those who learn from their failures are the ones who succeed in whatever they have disciplined their minds to focus on.

Try this practical exercise. Write down five new job skills you'd like to learn.

1._____
2._____
3._____
4._____
5._____

Review this list every day and imagine yourself learning these things. Research and develop a plan to learn these five skills and accomplish your goals.

You have greatness within you. If you are still reading this book, you are ready to make the leap of faith it takes to challenge yourself and become a better you.

"When one door of happiness closes, another opens; but often we look so long at the closed door that we do not see the one which has been opened for us."

-Helen Keller

CHAPTER 8

Believe that you can succeed.

You may already have the money you desire. You may have a successful career. You may have a house and white picket fence. Having these things may make you believe you don't need anything else.

Are you sure?

Are you sure you're comfortable and happy? Are you *sure* there isn't something you want or a position you aspire to? If you think you are satisfied with the status quo, you aren't being honest with yourself because it isn't human nature to be content with current circumstances.

Increasing your energy and drive will create momentum and take you to the next level. Let me ask: How many people in your inner circle are excited about life? How many positive people do you know? This is important because we absorb attitudes of the people around us; attitudes are contagious.

If you're around low-energy people, you will be a low-energy person. If the people around you are high-energy and excited about life, then you will have the same energy and excitement about your life.

Many are conditioned to believe life is a struggle. If you believe that, you're not going to be excited or energized. Therefore, you must alter your energy level if you want to change your outlook on the world.

You change your energy by changing your surroundings. This is not easy; it necessitates inner change. We all know that when we adjust to our mood, the outcome is not always good.

Energy, drive, and enthusiasm are the keys to creating a better atmosphere around you. You may have a friend who constantly complains about her family or job. You may have people around you who smoke weed and lie around the house all day doing nothing. You may have work where everyone is stressed and worried about a project, court case, or patient care and their enthusiasm is so low your energy drops to their level. They are not excited about their lives. Well, it is time to get fired up about life!

Accountability is everything. If we avoid it, we become weaker. Accountability will take us to the next level, but the more we strive to succeed, the harder it seems to reach that goal. You must feed on accountability, on discipline.

You must ask yourself, *What am I going to eat today— distraction or discipline?*

Before your day begins, you must believe the victory is already won. How do you do this? While easy, it takes discipline: Each night, write down how you see your day going tomorrow.

Sure, something may come up, but you don't want to greet the next day with just hope as your plan. You want strategy. Let's say you wake up at 5 a.m., go to the gym, and work out for 30 minutes. Then you eat something healthy, take a shower, iron your clothes, and arrive at work early. Because you committed your plan to paper, you knew what you were going to do that day.

If you do this every day, your enthusiasm and energy level will go through the roof; this is what happens when you get excited about life and hold yourself accountable for your decisions.

You must have a plan. Many people go through life without a plan and lack focus, then wonder why they end up in the same place day after day.

Before I realized I needed to change, my life was a struggle. My mother was murdered when I was young. I had a father, but I didn't allow him into my life. I ran the streets looking for ways to make easy money. I chose the wrong path and it led me away from everything that was good. Even my children.

I needed to make a choice. I knew that choice would change my life as well as the lives of everyone around me. After making the decision to change, I had to continue making choices, because with those first changes came more opportunities.

I don't know where you are in your life; your history, financial situation, or work and family environments, but I do know that if you have read this far, you are ready for your life to reach a higher level. Why not start right now?

"Challenges are what make life interesting, and overcoming them is what makes life meaningful."

-Joshua J. Marine

CHAPTER 9

. . . .

Every day, people are changing their lives.

They make more money than they've ever made before, or their family environment is much richer in love. Others sit around complaining instead of making a decision. Let me tell you what I mean when I say "make a decision": many people are playing the victim.

There may have been a time in your life where everything was going in your favor and, out of nowhere, it was all taken away from you. You may have had an amazing job and lost it. You may have believed you were in an amazing relationship but it ended. Someone really close to you may have passed away. Starting over has broken and discouraged you. These events can brainwash you into paralysis, making you feel you are a victim.

It is time to un-brainwash yourself. You'll never have a great financial future if you do not believe that you deserve it. You will never have an amazing family life if you do not believe that you deserve that amazing life. Without the proper mindset, your position in life will remain the same.

Whatever has happened in your life no longer matters; it is about what is going on *today* and in the future. As we move forward from today, decisions must be made. My mentor used to tell me, "Remove the stinky thinking."

A lot of successful business men have said they had to stop "small couch" thinking to be successful. Small couch thinking is when someone unconsciously discourages himself. They complain about everything and talk themselves out of becoming successful by settling for what they have. Stop doing that!

You must make a decision. How much time do you put into watching TV or playing online games? What do you think would happen if you stopped that and used the time to study, train, read a book, or listen to a motivational speaker?

Wow! Your life could change immensely.

What can you do when you run out of energy (punch drunk) and feel like doing nothing? You may feel powerless, discontent with where you are, bored with life, and find yourself on the couch watching life pass you by. It's time to control the spirit of the day. You may ask, "Yamuel, how do I control the spirit of the day?"

You begin by expanding your vision of yourself. If you invest effort into becoming a better you, you will see your self-investment manifest in your mental health, your business life, and your social life. You will begin to see a positive change in your relationships because your concentration is on putting yourself, your family, and your finances in a stronger position. Why accept less than you deserve—your destiny?

Sometimes, you accept less than you deserve because you have toxic, negative energy in your life, whether yours or other people's. Either way, it drains you.

You may believe those other people are a positive force. But could the truth be that their presence has forced you to give up on what you truly want? How many of your friends do you have intelligent conversations with? I'm talking about real life conversations that hold your attention and increase your desire to succeed.

You must understand this: If you want a better life, a better job, a better family life, you have to change yourself.

There is nothing wrong with seeking help. Often, change comes from being around someone who sees something in you that you cannot see in yourself. These people can take you to a place within yourself that you cannot go alone.

When you stop fighting for what you want in life, what you do not want will follow you. Your life, your family's lives, your finances, success—all depend on your choices.

You do not always get what you want. You get what you are, so you must become what you want. If you want a beautiful family, you must become a beautiful family member. You must build yourself up. What do you have to lose?

Go beyond your comfort zone to discover your awesomeness. You must be willing to give up who you currently are for who you want to become.

Bad habits? Give them up. Negative thinking? Give it up. The terrible romantic relationship must also go. Bad addictions, no matter what they are, must go.

However, you are not predestined for greatness. You must *choose* to be great in all that you do. You must test yourself daily to find out what you are made of. If you believe in yourself and have ambitious goals, you will find greatness all around you. It will be in everything you do. You are not predestined for greatness.

You were rich from the womb. Greatness is in your DNA and being successful is the only road your life can be based on. When you were born, you were a beautiful baby. Now, I *have* seen some ugly babies, but they were also designed for greatness.

Before a child could walk, they had to crawl. Before a child could speak, it had to cry. The child had to be raised and brought into adulthood.

Just as that child, you must train your mind to adjust to a new way of thinking. With ambitious goals comes more focused thinking.

Ask yourself:

- What are my strengths and weaknesses?
- What kind of person do I want to become to achieve the goals I want to achieve?
- What must I change to become who I want to become?

Make a commitment to honor everything you want to achieve. Do you believe that you would be in a better place than you are now if you had committed to discipline and self-improvement last month, last year? If the answer is "yes," it is time to make commitment a major force in your life. Let's start by setting goals to achieve a lifetime of greatness.

You already knew everything I have written in this book. You knew it because of who you are: someone with dreams and ambitions, someone who looks for ways to better themselves, their finances, and their family relationships. We are all students of life. A part of the growth process is learning how to be a better you.

I used to tell my son, "If you want to be a better basketball player, you have to practice like there is no tomorrow. Even after you practice with your team, you need to practice an hour afterward. Great basketball players put in more practice."

I practiced with my son to show him different moves to use on other players. The goal was to make him a better basketball player. He heard me, but he did not apply anything I said until he heard my exact words coming from someone else.

I could not understand why this was until my professor told me, "Everyone views the world differently. They can hear something from one person and hear it again from another, but the inspiration to change must come from within."

Your ideas will take you to greatness. Because you have a vision of yourself doing more and achieving more, you will no longer stress out or be financially challenged— because you were born rich.

You must also understand that you have something spiritual within; an empowering greatness. You can do more than you can imagine. A bigger life awaits you.

Consider how much money you want to earn this year or next year. Develop a number, a financial freedom number; the line that marks your freedom. Every time you look in the mirror think, *I'm not going to allow someone else to control my financial freedom.*

There are going to be distractions, challenges, and failures in your progress toward success. Hopefully, you will have family and friends alongside you to encourage you and motivate you, but some will try to discourage you. There will be people in your life who could help you but will not because they can't accept the new you, the one with dreams and ambitions. Don't allow another person's blindness stop you from realizing your dreams. You want to live for your dreams, not your fears.

Make sure your foundation of self is firm and grounded. Begin with thinking about your goals, dreams, and your finances. Then develop effective communication skills.

What is your story? Others want to know. To effectively relay your story to them, work on your communication skills so that your words will not go in one ear and out the other.

You must also believe in your abilities. When you believe in yourself, you'll be able to create a better future for yourself and those you contact along your path. You must know it is possible.

It is possible to be and do everything you put your mind to because you see it in yourself every day when you look in the mirror.

"Live as if you were to die tomorrow. Learn as if you were to live forever."

-Mahatma Gandhi

CHAPTER 10

You can do it.

It is time to discipline your mind by doing what you know you can do, if you have an idea, you can do it. If you have a dream, you can, and will, do it. If you have a goal, you can achieve it.

You may ask, "How do you know this, Yamuel?"

Because you were born with a rich mind and a rich personality. You were born with greatness inside you, and the awesomeness in you radiates everywhere you go!

It doesn't matter where you have been in life. It does not matter if you're homeless, rich or poor, employed or unemployed. The only thing that can stop you from achieving your dreams and aspirations is YOU.

I would love to tell you the road to success is going to be easy, but it is going to be a fight. You will come up against many challenges, so you must be ready. Some will lose friends and feel defeated. You must be prepared to stand. If anyone ever told you life is a yellow brick road if you just do this or that was misleading you; not preparing you for that one incident that can change your life.

When we believe that nothing bad will happen to us because everything is going so well, we are setting ourselves up for failure. You are a winner and must think like a winner at all times. Every moment and step on your path to success must be a calculated step. Your mind must hope for the best but prepare for the worst.

Being prepared for worst case scenarios will keep you focused. If a door closes, another will open. If you lose a job, you will get another one, maybe even a better one. The only thing that can stop you from success is you. Become a decisive person and spend more energy on a solution than worrying about the challenges that arise in your life. If you really want to be transformed, you have to live an intentional life.

Your life has a purpose. One of the greatest issues in America is that so many people believe their life has no purpose. Because of this, they lower their level of living and thinking and accept jobs that limit life. Just because you were raised in a lower-class household does not mean you are destined to mentally and physically live in such an environment for the rest of your life. You have a purpose with a divine touch.

Whatever job you do have, complete it to the best of your ability. When you have an incredible work ethic, you will be seen and promoted.

If we look at the most successful men and women in the world we will find that they all have something in common: a routine. They never failed to prepare because they knew that they would be preparing to fail. They strengthened their minds by reading and studying the business they were in, but most of all, they were great listeners. They listened to other speakers who told of their failures and successes and learned from them, preparing for their own failures to arise on the path to success.

Winning from Start to Finish is a guide to prepare you for both your success and your failures. You must understand failure is not fatal if you learn from it. That failure, if properly utilized, will strengthen your mindset and skill set. There is no limit to your success once you have found something in your life that gives you a strong sense of competence. And, that something is YOU!

You can't make a basket unless you shoot the ball, you can't hit a home run unless you swing. You must assume the ball *will* go into the net when you shoot and that you will hit a home run when you swing.

You must be persistent in everything you do to achieve success. Your thought must be, *I deserve this and I am going to have it.* Take what you deserve—be the best you in all that you do. If you wait until your children grow up or that perfect relationship appears, nothing will happen. If you wait for society to change, nothing will happen. Take a chance and walk by faith, not by sight.

You can do it! Make that difference in your life now. Do not hold back the gift that God has given to the world . . . YOU!

Acknowledgments

I want to give special thanks to Daryl Richeson, my general manager, for encouraging me to write a book titled *Winning from Start to Finish*. As a general manager, he has always encouraged people to give their best in all that they do. His drive and empowering presence has kept me focused on writing, especially when I believed I had writer's block. I would also like to thank Diana Bogert who helped me with my writing ideas and brainstorming, Ylianna Walters who helped format this book, Editorial Consultants: Heather Pendley, developmental editor from Reedsy.com, Allen Taylor, chief content officer @ Taylored Content LLC, and Girlou Sumalinog layout artist.

Thanks also to my children who have influenced my writing and have been my greatest motivators. My goal has always been to show them it doesn't matter where you have been in life; today is what matters, so live like there is no tomorrow.

Most importantly, I give thanks to God who gave me the words to write. Without a spiritual foundation with

Him, none of this work would have been possible. And, yes, thanks to the one and only Alphonse Bradley Sr.

My father told me, "Your past does not define you."

Thanks everyone. Without your support, this book would not have been written.

www.ingramcontent.com/pod-product-compliance
Lightning Source LLC
Chambersburg PA
CBHW071849020426
42331CB00007B/1919